KEEPING
GOD
COMPANY

This is the fourth collection of Trevor Dennis's stories. *Speaking of God* was published by Triangle in 1992, *Imagining God* by SPCK in 1997 and *The Three Faces of Christ* by Triangle in 1999. He started preaching through storytelling in the 1970s, when he was a school chaplain, but most of his stories since, including the ones contained in this book, have been designed primarily for adults. For nearly twelve years he taught Old Testament studies at Salisbury and Wells Theological College, and SPCK has published four books of his exploring Old Testament passages. At the beginning of 1994 he joined the staff of Chester Cathedral, where he is now Vice Dean. He is married to Caroline, who teaches dyslexic children, and they have four children.

KEEPING
GOD
COMPANY

Trevor Dennis

First published in Great Britain in 2002 by
SPCK
Holy Trinity Church
Marylebone Road
London NW1 4DU

British Library Cataloguing-in-Publication Data

A catalogue record for this book is available from the British Library

ISBN 0-281-05464-9

Typeset by Pioneer Associates, Perthshire
Printed in Great Britain by
Omnia Books, Glasgow

For Sister Elizabeth Clare, CHN,
who keeps God company and
helps so many do the same.

CONTENTS

INTRODUCTION AND
ACKNOWLEDGEMENTS

Over the past 25 years I have sometimes preached through storytelling, where the story is the sermon and fills it entirely, and in recent years I have developed a meditative style that has led me to make more frequent use of short lines and brought me closer to poetry. I relish the freedom such preaching gives me, freedom of thought, of imagination and of language. It allows me to play with my memories and experience, play, also, with the biblical text, its imagery and metaphors, its bright storytelling and startling poetry. That play is not mischievous nor casual, but represents an attempt on my part to let the Bible live afresh, to give my experiences and memories some meaning for others, and to put some colour into God's cheeks.

Most of the pieces in this book were first preached in Chester Cathedral, where I am on the staff, though some were written for other congregations, or for people on retreats I was leading.

Those who are unfamiliar with my work will quickly notice the frequency with which I use feminine pronouns of God. When it comes to God I talk more easily of 'she' and 'her' than of 'he' and 'his'. I am not trying to be different, or clever. I am well aware of the fact that the Bible never uses such pronouns, though it does sometimes compare God to a human mother, or a midwife, or a mother bird brooding her young. I realize also, of course, that God is no more female than male, that God is indeed far beyond the human, and far beyond the tight limitations of our human language and imagination. Yet over the years I have grown increasingly impatient with all the language drawn from the world of men of power which still we apply to God with such relish, and the feminine talk has come to evoke more successfully for me the mystery, the intimacy, and the love of the God I know.

I have frequently been surprised by the impact my pieces have had on some people, and equally surprised by the interest SPCK has continued to show in them. This is the fourth collection they have published, and I am especially grateful to their Senior Editor, Alison Barr, for encouraging me to submit more pieces, for the thoughtful and courteous way she made her selection from those I sent her, and for the intelligence and carefulness with which she has handled the turning of them into a book.

I owe a huge debt, also, to Sister Elizabeth Clare of the Community of the Holy Name, Sister Liz, as she is known to all her friends. For a few years running up to Christmas 2000, with other members of the Community, Liz lived and worked at the Retreat House in the Cathedral precincts here in Chester, just a hundred yards from where my wife and I live. During that time we agreed to act as spiritual companions for one another ('spiritual directors' will not do, since neither of us seeks to direct the other). We have continued seeing each other on a regular basis, although the Community has had to pull out of the Retreat House and leave it to a new Warden to run, and Liz herself has gone to another Community house a hundred miles away. Sometimes we find that rare person who can show us clearly a deeper way of living, remind us of what is important, and lead us further into the heart of God. Liz for me is such a person. She has no idea, I am sure, of what she has given me and continues to give me. With much gratitude and love I have dedicated this book to her. It is not enough.

KEEPING GOD COMPANY

The little collection of stories and meditations that make up this book is dedicated to Sister Elizabeth Clare, CHN, or Sister Liz, as I and all her friends call her. I have already spoken in the Introduction of my larger debt to her. For this first piece, I owe her particular gratitude, for she is the nun who appears in it. She told me the story with which it begins. She had met a young woman at Euston Station, when she was sitting outside in the sunshine waiting for a train. The remarkable vision of God 'needing our companionship' also comes from her, and first burst upon her when she was lying in a hospital bed after a painful operation on one of her feet had failed. The wonderful phrase, 'keeping God company', which gives the piece and the whole collection its title, is one she gave me in the course of yet another conversation. Without her, therefore, this piece would not even have begun. All I have done is reflect upon what she gave me.

Liz gave me permission to use her words before I preached them in Chester Cathedral, and she has again given me permission to include them in this book. For that, too, I thank her.

'God improves on acquaintance, you know.'
That was what she said.
A parting gift to a stranger
who had asked her for money,
attracted by her nun's habit,
without appreciating its poverty,
who had got into deeper conversation
than she had bargained for.

'God improves on acquaintance.'
Was the gift accepted?
We do not know.
There was no answer made.
Can be no answer.
It's true, that's all.

Because you do, God,
improve on acquaintance, I mean.
'The fear of the Lord is the beginning of wisdom,'
the Bible says.
Not if 'fear' means fear,
or touching our forelocks,
or putting on a good show,
or terror.

Not even (can this be true?)
if it means reverence.
For you don't want our reverence, God,
any more than we wish to be revered by our friends.
You want our love.

And our companionship.
My friend, the nun, said that, too.
'God needs our companionship,' she said.
'It's all a matter of keeping God company,' she said.
I've never forgotten her.

It sounds absurd, God, doesn't it,
this talk of companionship,
let alone you needing it.
Just happens to be true, that's all.

It sounds so arrogant.
How can we be so important to you?
How can we make such a difference?
How might you be lonely without us,
as if you had no companions
till we came along,
so very late in the days of creation?

But all we can know
is how you relate to us,
and that is hard enough.
We cannot tell what pleasure
lichens have with you,
or ravens on cathedral towers,
let alone beds of sandstone.

All we know
is that your love for us,
and for all things,
is utterly compelling,
at times quite overwhelming,
and those are the times
when we are most alive,
most generous and creative,
most human.

And all we know
is when your love is not returned,
and we busy ourselves with other things,
or turn our backs,
or get religious,
or self-conscious,
or fidgety,

then, in truth,
in strange, nonsensical truth,
you are left alone,
embracing nothing.

We turn in your direction
when first we feel your pain.
Then we are compelled
to open our arms
to receive you.

Once we thought
it was your job to embrace us, God.
So we waited for you,
and knew too often
our own loneliness.

We did not see
that what we called our search for you
was but a part of our perennial preoccupation with
    ourselves.
We felt our own disappointment,
but not yours.

It was when we looked over the top of our prayer
that suddenly we saw you,
saw you afar off,
and filled with compassion,
ran to meet you
and put our arms about you
and kissed you.

We had thought
it was meant to be the other way around.

That was before we felt your pain,
and saw you couldn't move.

You improve on acquaintance, God.
We could do with some improvement of our own.

Keeping you company might do the trick.

ONCE GOD SANG

I preached this in Chester Cathedral at a Festival Evensong during the Chester Summer Music Festival. I wished to celebrate the creativity of composers and musicians, and link it to the creativity of God.

In the beginning,
before the heavens and the earth,
when God and eternity were quite alone,
there was silence

and in the silence of that dark void
God sang.

There was no bang,
no explosion,
no violence,
only a song,
a love song
straight from the heart of God.
God sang out her soul,
sang this universe into being.

She did not need to roll up her sleeves for creation.
She had no fight on her hands,
no slaying of dragons,
no splitting of monsters.
Only a song that took its flight,
soared and circled,
curled the fingers of its wings,

twisted wide its tail,
somersaulted,
closed and dropped and swept again
to turn and turn around the new-made stars.

The universe was and is
God's oratorio,
and this round earth
one delicate aria for soprano voice
(God's pitch is not as deep and thunderous
as we are too often told to imagine).

We human beings
took form late in the song, at bar 99.
By then the waves were sighing on rock and sand,
swinging back and forth to the moon's quiet call;
strange rainbow lights were shimmering the northern
    sky,
and whales had composed their song cycles;
wolves were answering the swaying canticle of the trees,
while nightingales were reducing all to tears.

So already,
before we slid upon this earth,
before we stood and lost our stoop,
God's aria had become an Hallelujah Chorus.

God gave us parts to sing,
our own parts,
that no ocean, no wind, no other creature could get its
tongue around.
Lustily we sang it for a spell,
till other ideas came into our heads.

Sometimes we closed our ears
and chose to sing a line of our own making,
out of key, out of tune.
We do it still.
Sometimes we yelled raw from the throat,
barked out ugly melody
that had no measure to it,
and warned all else,
including God,
to fall impossibly in step.
We do it still.
Sometimes we left the chorus lines behind,
built a high podium,
and took a baton as heavy as a truncheon
with which to beat all else,
including God,
into submission.
We do it still.

Yet sometimes,
we sat as still as God
beside a nightingale bush,
and went away and made violins.
And sometimes,
we kept our ears open
to the stars,
to the deep calling of the earth,
to the wide song of the oceans,
went and covered paper
with lines and dots,
writing, 'To the greater glory of God', at the end,
and handed the paper
to those who could take the dots
and turn them from their very souls.

And then, oh, then,
even the nightingales would pause,
the wolves and trees would cease from their duets,
the very stars would hush,
and God would hold out hands to us,
no longer pinned with nails,
but freed for dance,
and she would sway and turn
and swish her skirts
and bend her neck,
and sing with us
and still would sing,
and earth and heaven would then be one,
to call it 'resurrection'.

We do it still.
We do it still!

Oh, let us do it still!

A TIME OF WAITING

*This story draws on the history of the Palestinian village of Kafir
Bir'im in the Galilee hills, whose inhabitants were expelled by
the new Israeli authorities in 1948 'for security reasons'. The
Israeli Supreme Court subsequently ruled in favour of their return,
and they were told to go back on Christmas Day 1951. As they
approached the village, however, Israeli soldiers dynamited and
bulldozed their homes, leaving only the church standing.*

*There was no massacre at Kafir Bir'im, but at the village of
Al-Dawayima near Hebron that same year nearly one hundred
people, including women and children, were killed. With story-
teller's licence I have put together the stories of the two villages,
and used my imagination to paint the details.*

*I could have made the story darker still. On 9 April 1948,
245 men, women and children died at Deir Yassin, just outside
Jerusalem, killed by members of the Zionist Irgun and Stern
gangs.*

'What are you waiting for, my friend? Advent is a time of
waiting. What are you waiting for? The sound of a baby's cry,
breaking the silence of a winter's night? That small sound of
God, breaking through the noise of the world? Something to
comfort you, to make you feel for a moment that all is well?

'I too am waiting. Like you.

'Some people rush around while they are waiting for
Christmas. Advent is such a busy time. There's no time to think
of anything except what on earth to buy uncle this, or what
not to send to sister that, for last year's bottle of cheap scent was
a disaster and started off her asthma, as she was quick to write
and say.

'I too am waiting.

'Some people manage to stop still and wait, at least for a spell. For them Advent becomes like sitting in a hide watching for the bittern to leave the cover of the reeds; or like turning, looking for the bride to come up the aisle; or like longing for the nine months to be up, for the child to leave the womb and come to light, come to crying, come to holding, come to tears of relief and joy. Yes, most especially like waiting for a child to be born.

'For in Advent we are all waiting, even if we are rushing round like mad things, driven to distraction by a world which has taken over Christmas without knowing what it's for. We are all waiting to hear God's voice in that baby's cry, to see God's tears in that baby's eyes, to feel God's skin in the softness of that baby's cheek held tight against our own. And beyond Advent we wait to see that same God smile and walk and run and play on this wide earth and talk and laugh and make us proud.

'While you wait, I am waiting, also, waiting, this Advent, for someone to take notice of me. Then for some justice. Those who already have justice speak of mercy beyond it. For me justice will do to be going on with. Oh, I do not ask for those who came to our village all those years ago to get their just deserts. I am not interested in that. My God has no interest in any of us getting our just deserts, so I don't see why I should be. I'm not interested in that sort of justice, but in the justice that means someone takes notice of me, and does something about it, or allows me to do something, to recover my belonging, my living, my place, my dignity, my purpose, my hope.

'They came to our village at night. By the time the sun was up nearly a hundred bodies lay crumpled on the ground, with the life shot or stabbed out of them, men, women and children. My little sister was among them, and my mother. They had fallen together, and had died with their arms round each other. My father, my brother and I had run, scattering into the olive groves with the rest who had managed to escape.

'Three years later they told us we could go home. It was Christmas Day. Christmas Day! We were going back. Not just us, but many families, some of them complete, some like ours. As we walked down the familiar dirt road, our hearts were beating fast. It was where we belonged. The place was ours, and had made us what we were. Yet what would we find? The houses had been empty all this time. And after that dreadful night we'd not been able to go back to bury our dead. What kind of burials had my mother, my baby sister, and all the rest of them been given? We all wondered that, though we said nothing to one another.

'We never found out. As we came near the edge of the village, soldiers came out from under the trees and blocked our way. Before we could show them our papers we heard the sound of bulldozers, and then the explosion of dynamite. We stood there in the road for the next few hours, at gunpoint, and watched as they blew our houses to bits, or pushed and shoved them into piles of rubble. Then they told us to leave.

'They left the church standing, but there is no-one there to ring its bell now. You will not find even the name of our village on any official map. It is not there any more. It has been wiped off the face of the earth.

'But they cannot wipe our memories clean. They cannot make us forget. They cannot stop us dreaming. And as long as we live we will keep waiting, until we die, or until someone notices us.

'So I am waiting also this Advent. Like you, my friend, I am waiting.

'You ask where my village was. When I was a child I could see the Sea of Galilee from the roof of our house, just a few miles to the south. I lived, I still live in the land you call the Holy Land. And so it is. But I would like it to be known as the Just Land also.

'There will be those in your own villages, your towns and cities, who are waiting for justice, too, this Advent. Perhaps you are among them. Waiting for someone to take notice of you. Waiting for a Christmas to remember, not like the one when we tried to return to our homes, of course, but a Christmas worthy of the name.

'I wish you a happy Christmas, my friend. I will pray for you. Remember me.'

4

ANNUNCIATION

Luke's famous story of the appearance of the angel Gabriel to Mary of Nazareth is not the first annunciation story in the Bible. God appears to the already pregnant Hagar in Genesis 16, and again to the wife of Manoah in Judges 13 (she is left unnamed in Judges, but later rabbis called her Eluma), and then, in 1 Samuel 1, there is the equally poignant story of Hannah, a woman desperate for a child. Luke will have had such stories in his mind when he wrote the opening chapters of his Gospel.

Luke averts our gaze from the potential catastrophe of Mary's pregnancy. Matthew, in his story of the annunciation to Joseph in the first chapter of his Gospel, is more open about it, though not as blunt as he might be. Yet the stories of both Matthew and Luke are about disgrace turned to grace, grace for all humankind, for evermore. Properly understood, they are not about a virgin birth – that doctrine came later in the Christian Church. They are about a far larger miracle, one that reaches to the heart of God and God's eternal creativity.

In times far distant,
almost beyond our horizon,
and out of Luke's reach, also,
so it would seem,
God himself appeared
for annunciation.

He came himself to Hagar's desert,
by the well at Beer-lahai-roi.
Hagar saw God,
saw *God*,

and named him, too!
God left Hagar's well
proudly bearing a new identity,
a new name,
her name for him,
her mark upon him,
for ever and ever, Amen.

God came himself,
wrapped in awe,
to the wife of Manoah,
to tell of the birth of her son,
slipped into the house
when Manoah was not looking,
met her a second time,
most outrageously,
out in the open,
when again Manoah was off the scene!

By the time we reach Luke's story,
God has long ceased walking the earth, it seems.
Cut off in heaven,
he must send an angel,
trailing his divinity.

Yet Mary is as amazed as Hagar was,
as unnerved as Eluma,
rabbi-named wife of Manoah.
Gabriel has his own name, for sure,
in all the paintings his own wings also,
and private disc of light about his head.
Yet surely 'Gabriel' is another name for God.
Surely Hagar and Eluma both tell us that.

So God himself comes to Nazareth,
unseen, unheeded by all
except this young woman.

She is not ready for him,
she is not ready for a child, either.
She is only betrothed,
not yet married.
A child too soon will spell ruin,
for her, for Joseph,
for their families.
If she is pregnant now,
her young form will swell with disgrace,
and bring forth disaster.
She cannot contemplate a child.
Not yet.

And yet
this Gabriel-God comes to speak
of pregnancy, of birth,
of a son, of naming,
of greatness, thrones and kingdoms,
and all the while
can tell of nothing but grace!
He calls her
'the graced one',
graced, engraced, all-graced.
He tells her
she has found grace already;
he has sheltered her,
will surely shelter her
beneath the wide wings of his divinity.
They will be enough to hide her from contempt.

More than that,
much more,
the wings of God
will be the coverings of her palanquin.
'The Holy Spirit will come upon you,
and the power of the Most High will
    overshadow you.'
This is coronation talk!
Language fit from ancient times
for a king,
new-minted for a queen.
Disgrace is turned quite all to grace!
Her son
(her son!)
will be the son of God!
She will ride in his entourage!
'Here I am,' she says,
'the Lord's slave,'
meaning no humiliation,
but honour, and power,
and fine reflected glory.
For Moses also,
of shining face,
was 'the slave of God',
and Abraham, Isaac, Jacob, too,
Joshua, David, the prophets,
and a woman who came so close to annunciation,
the mother of Samuel, the king-maker,
Hannah.
'Here I am, the Lord's slave.'
These words put Mary in fine company!

The empire of distant Rome
in which she lives

is run by an emperor's slaves.
She counts herself in much higher company!
She is too good for Augustus!
She walks *God's* corridors of power;
shares *God's* secrets.
She is God's confidante,
the bearer of his child!
For her son,
the son that spelled such ruin,
will be the Son of God,
grace, engraced, beyond grace.

Give her a note,
and this young woman
will sing a queen's song,
that we will call 'Magnificat'!

And when she is done,
and her voice has died away,
then we must listen for the rustle of God's wings,
see their shadow enfolding us,
feel again the warmth,
the eternal safety
beneath their shelter,
smell the sweet scent of God's grace,
and taste and see
in a disc of bread and a sip of wine
how good,
how very good,
the Lord is.

For here too,
as once in Nazareth,
as always in God's company,
disgrace is turned quite all to grace.

5

THE HERMIT

This is a story about the birth of Christ, and draws upon Matthew's story of the visit of the Wise Men. But it has clear reference, also, to the Moses stories from Exodus, particularly to the story in Exodus 33 of God hiding Moses in a cleft of the rock of Mount Sinai, and telling him he would see his 'retreating' as he passed him by ('retreating' is possibly a better translation of the Hebrew in Exodus 33.23 than the more usual 'back'). The story of the capture and destruction of Jericho in Joshua 6 plays another part in this piece, together with the story of Elijah being fed in the desert in 1 Kings 19, as well as my own memories of the Judean desert and of seeing a golden eagle in Scotland being mobbed by a pair of ravens. As this mixture indicates, I have exercised a great deal of freedom in the composition of this story.

The wise men had lost their way.

It was no light matter. The ground was harsh and dry. A few small flowers grew precariously among the stones, but there was nothing to eat. Only thorns and thistles. Eden and its plenty were left far behind. The heat pressed them hard, threatening to squeeze the life out of them. It was a long time since they had last found water. Now it was all gone. They had come a long way, only to die, it seemed, among these desiccated hills.

The last three nights had been cloudy. They had not been able to see the stars. Their leading light had disappeared. They were within ten miles of Bethlehem, but they did not know it. It would not have helped them if they had, for they did not understand it was their destination. All their wisdom had brought them only to this, a dry wadi in an empty, God-forsaken land.

It was late afternoon and the air was even more hostile than usual. They felt faint. Vultures circled easily above them as if waiting for them to collapse.

Then one of them spotted a cave the far side of the wadi, half hidden behind some rocks. It would be cool in there, at least, and pleasantly dark, a better place to wait for death. They scrambled up to it, and fell exhausted on its floor. They closed their eyes, not sure whether they would open them again.

When they did, they could not believe them. Jars of milk were standing there, loaves of bread and baskets piled with dates and figs. There was wild honey too.

'A miracle!' they cried.

'No, breakfast.'

Startled, they looked round. An old man stood at the entrance of the cave. 'Welcome to my home,' he said. He bowed stiffly.

'You live here?'

'Yes.'

'How do you survive?'

'Where did you find the milk and all this food?'

'Such abundance! We could find nothing.'

'I'm used to the desert. I know its secrets. I've been here for many centuries.' He smiled and bowed to them again.

Clearly he was mad, but there was no madness in the feast he had provided.

'You have saved our lives.'

'That's what I'm here for. I've had enough of death and killing.'

He gazed out across the wadi. Two ravens were mobbing an eagle. Their elegant acrobatics lasted some minutes, and the old man watched them intently till they disappeared.

'I saw his retreating,' he said quietly, still looking across the valley. 'The other side of the Jordan, high up in the cleft of the rock of heaven, I saw his retreating. I had asked to see his glory,

but that was too much to ask, of course. You cannot see God
and live, so they say. Yet I saw his retreating, and later, at
Jericho, I saw him in full flight. They thought I had died the
other side of the river, but they were wrong. I came down
Mount Nebo and crossed the Jordan at night, like Jacob at the
Jabbok, on my own. I was not far behind them. I saw what
happened at Jericho. Armed with the fire and sword of God,
they burned the crops, cut down the palm trees, then sent the
troops in. I could hear the screaming. It went on for ever, and
still I hear it in my dreams. But it was not so terrible as the
silence that followed. The ancient springs of the town ran
thick with blood. And my God was covered in the stuff, roaring
victory.

'That's when I turned my back on him. So much for his
glory! I had seen more than enough of it. I had thought I had
known him on Sinai, got close to him, as close as anyone might
this side of death. But he had deceived me. He was no more
than a common thug. I prefer eagles and ravens to God any day.'

The wise men knew him now, and knew he was not mad.
They stood in the darkness of the cave, unable to speak.

At last one of them said quietly, 'We have come in search of
him.'

'Oh have you now!' The old man laughed. 'And you have
found me instead. What cruel luck! I cannot lead you to God.
Nor would I wish to, if I could.'

'Perhaps we can take you there instead.'

'I have seen enough, thank you.'

'I think not,' the wise man persisted. 'Look, it is dark, and the
clouds have gone. We must be going. You have saved our lives.
Come with us on this last stage of our journey. You missed
your God at Jericho. You missed him, and mistook another for
him. The god you saw there is an old imposter, who still finds
his followers, alas. You were once the friend of the God that is
good and true. Come with us, and you will be so again.'

The old man shook his head, yet, fearing they might get lost again, went with them all the same.

The sky was crystal clear. The pages of heaven were once more wide open for them to read. In the small hours of that famous night they came to Bethlehem, reaching the place for which the wise men had taken their journey. They knelt and bowed their heads, stretching out their gifts.

Moses did not kneel. Behind them, on the edges of that small space, he remained standing. He had always stood before his God. The child's mother, recognizing him, beckoned him forward. He hesitated, then came and took the child in his arms. It was many years, many centuries indeed, since he had held a baby. How soft his skin was! This God of his was so small, so fragile seeming! He held him tight, then put him against his cheek. All the love, so long forgotten, came flooding back and engulfed him.

'My little friend,' he whispered. 'Do you recall the song you taught me, the song we used to sing together on Sinai? Such times we had!'

The music of a strange song, lines from another world that seemed long gone, filled the air.

There was a pause, and the wise men looked up from where they knelt, hoping for another verse. They saw Joseph rocking the child to sleep, singing him a lullaby. That was all.

HIDDEN TREASURE

In 1997 major work was done on the nave of Chester Cathedral, where I work. Underfloor heating was installed, new stone pavers laid, and new chairs introduced. While the work on the floor was progressing, two members of the Cathedral Estate team were high above on a scaffolding platform, cleaning the Victorian wooden roof. After them came the decorators, painting a limewash over the wooden ribs to make them look like the red sandstone of the walls, and gilding the bosses. The effect was so striking and so beautiful, I decided to preach about it. But I did not wish to preach just about a roof. I wanted also to speak of Jesus of Nazareth. This piece is the result.

The trees were carefully chosen. Oaks. Wood that would harden to iron, given enough time. Wood full of colour, shades of fox, of gold, lined and ringed with age.

It was cut and shaped, carved into planks, into ribs, into round, heavy weighted bosses. Beneath the knock of the chisel faces emerged, moustached faces of men known to the carvers, leaves, animals, and even the shapes of God.

Thus, through the skill and care of those who had an eye for wood and who could see what it might become, some cart-loads of trees became a roof for a cathedral.

Those in charge of the operations thought it best to hide the lines of the wood beneath a flat, dark stain, to make it look more of their time and less of the ancient time of the trees.

The fine intricacies of the carvings they stained also, and made them so dark they could not be seen any more, except by the pigeons that occasionally flew in through a hole in one of the windows, and caused the vergers such problems.

Down below other men shovelled coke into curious round stoves, or burned smoking candles, and the dust of the town somehow found its way in, also, and layered itself onto the soot rising inexorably from below. The fine roof became heavy, dark, pressing down upon the walls and upon those who knelt in prayer.

Two men found the wood again. They began to wash the planks and ribs. The water in their buckets turned the colour of tar. The stain washed off in their hands, and the time-honoured lines of the trees were seen once more. They took a hosepipe to the bosses, and exposed their shy splendour, too.

Yet some were still not content. The roof they discovered up there, high on the scaffolding platform, was so startling. Those who would sit or walk or pray far beneath, how could they be shown its glories in all their fullness? What might the roof become, beyond its new-found cleanliness? They decided to lime the ribs, and gild the bosses with leaves of thin gold. They would make the ribs seem like stone. They would make them stand proud of the wood, weave fine patterns, create curving, interlinking arches, springing from wall to wall, repeating end to end. They would raise the roof, making the space tall, lifting the eye and the heart. And they would make the bosses shine, gleaming rows of them, stars in the building's firmament.

And so they did.

Those who walked beneath and those who came to pray realized for the first time what treasure they had, treasure long hidden, not buried beneath their feet and now unearthed, but concealed above their heads till then by years of dirt, by flattening stain, by lack of lime and dearth of thin gold leaf.

ᐤᐤ

A man lived once in Palestine who found hidden treasure wherever he went and polished it bright with the love of God till it shone. Bartimaeus was a nuisance, but not to him. Mary of Magdala was shut off by terrifying illness, but he was not afraid. Zacchaeus was a pest, an unscrupulous, calculating little thief, acting for a foreign power, but not to him. He saw through the madness of the man among the tombs, and uncovered his sanity. Confronted with a paralysed man, he perceived at once the guilt that held him fast, set him free with forgiveness, and made him walk away as tall as Hercules, carrying his bed. Not for a moment did he believe he could be made unclean by the blood of a desperate woman who touched his clothes in a crowd, hoping not to be noticed. He felt her need as if it was his own, and recognized immediately her courage and her trust. After that she was able to be a part of the crowd again, instead of having to hide away in the darkness of her room.

He could not despise anyone, or think them drab or cheap. Contempt was beyond his nature.

These, the ones whose true worth he knew, whose bright treasure he uncovered, lit his way to Calvary. Their lamps, unlike the lamps of his other friends, did not splutter out into darkness. They ringed the hill of his death with tiny flames, like stars. The soldiers did not see them. They had come for the marriage of heaven and earth. They had come to light the bridegroom's way with their love. A few days later on in the ceremonies they wound their way in slow procession to his tomb and found it already blazing with light. Then their wedding celebrations began in earnest! Earth and heaven were united, and no-one could put them asunder.

Earth in heaven, heaven on earth. Heaven on earth wherever we look. That is what the man from Palestine taught. Hidden treasure, waiting for our finding, waiting for our noticing, waiting for us to uncover its glories in all their fullness.

Alleluia!

The stories of Jesus' resurrection concern God's unexpected triumph over the forces of violence, chaos, evil and death. All four of the Evangelists place stories early in their Gospels that anticipate that final victory. One of them is the story of the Calming of the Storm, for a stormy sea had been used by storytellers and poets for millennia as a symbol of the forces of evil and chaos, such as only God could control (it appears in that guise in places in the Old Testament). Thus, when we reach Luke 8.22–25 and his version of the Calming of the Storm (my text for this particular piece), we enter what we might call a resurrection story. The trouble is, it is a resurrection without a crucifixion. Knowing what we know from the later chapters of Luke's Gospel, and from the others, too, we cannot help thinking the story of the Calming of the Storm makes things seem too easy. There can be no resurrection without a death, nor victory of that kind without seeming defeat. In my rewriting of the story of the Storm I have brought back the death, and the apparent catastrophe.

I have also taken the chance at one point to reflect further on what is happening in Jesus' land, and in particular on what the Palestinians have to endure. Jesus himself was a Jew, of course, and yet his situation and that of his friends and followers was much closer to that of the Palestinians today, than to that of the Jewish Israelis.

The quotation near the end of the piece is from The Song of Songs 8.6–7a.

One day he got into a boat.
One day he left behind the Holy of Holies,

crept out, carefully keeping the curtain for the time
    being intact,
left silently, so the priests would not hear his going,
left his temple an empty abattoir,
took heaven with him,
and got into a boat,
found himself a cushion at the stern,
and went to sleep.

He dreamed uneasily of an ark
rocking in its tiny loneliness
on an ocean of troubles.
Swaying gently on the water's gleaming skin,
he knew too well the monstrous cancers hiding
    in its depths;
he knew their bids for power,
their dark intentions.

His friends were not oblivious to them, either.
They were fishermen, after all.
They knew this sea,
were familiar with its tantrums.
And they had seen too much on land for comfort,
become too used to others' violence and abuse,
known the dead weight of being so near the
    bottom of the pile.
They were not simple;
they had won their tiny victories from time to time.
But how can you fight with sticks and stones
against an enemy who drives you down with
    tons of steel,
or, whirring noisily, puts you up against a wall
and shoots you from the sky?
How can you win the day

against their herding you like pigs over the cliffs
   of destitution,
when they stop your food and take your water
and do whatever in their bitterness and fear they like?

His friends were not simple,
nor oblivious.
They knew too well the lurking terrors of the world;
they knew you never knew
when next they might erupt
to smite the calm,
to put you up against a wave
and smash the living daylights out of you.

It was no surprise for them
when the storm so suddenly began.
That did not mean that they could hide their fear,
or take it on the chin,
lie down and die,
content once more to drown.
'Master, master, we are perishing!' they cried,
and cried with all their strength
against the mocking of the wind,
the bitter hurling of the waves.

'Master, master, we are perishing!' they cried,
and still he slept,
dreaming of an ark floating upside-down.

As the last wave curled itself to pounce,
they woke him from his trance.
And so at last he stood and faced the storm,
and looked it darkly in the eye,
as now it gathered all its strength against the boat,
and snapped it quite in two.

Then silence fell upon the lake.
No yell of wind,
no thump of wave,
no 'Master we are perishing!'
Kind planks and jagged shards of mast
cajoled them gently to the shore,
till once again they stood on land
and shook the water from their eyes.

There was no sign of him.
He was quite gone.
The waters must have taken him.
Those ancient monsters of the deep
must have snatched him for their own,
and he must be their prisoner.
There would be no stopping them now.

They did not hear the angels sing.
Only the owls,
and shepherds keeping watch over their flocks
    by night
caught hearing of their ancient words:
    'Set me as a seal upon your heart,
    as a seal upon your arm;
    for love is strong as death,
    passion fierce as the grave.
    Many waters cannot quench love,
    neither can floods drown it.'

Not till after Golgotha would his friends hear
    that song,
and then they would at last understand,
and, understanding,
be no more afraid.

8 THE MEAL

I wrote this piece for an Agape, a Eucharist set in the context of a three course meal. A parish church in Chester had asked me to preside and preach. The story of the Feeding of the Five Thousand in Matthew 14 was an obvious choice for the Gospel.

Who is our narrator here? She inhabits the stories of Exodus, for she has crossed the Red Sea, she has walked to Mount Sinai, she has heard God's voice sounding from the summit, she has watched as Moses, and, on one occasion Aaron, Nadab and Abihu and seventy of the elders (see Exodus 24.9–11), climbed the steep rock of the mountain, she has eaten the manna, and has given up her jewellery to help make the Golden Calf. Yet she lives in the land of Jesus, she is in the crowd in the story of the Feeding of the Five Thousand, and she knows too well what Roman occupation means. She even knows what it is like for the Palestinians of our own day to live in an occupied land, that very same occupied land. She does not belong to one particular age, nor one particular people. She belongs wherever and whenever there is hunger and oppression and a desperate need of God's bounty.

Long ago, when we were children,
kicking and screaming on God's hip,
when Egyptian brutality had been broken to pieces
and cast upon the waters
for dark Leviathan to rise and eat his fill,
the desert was strewn with manna against our starving.

We came as far as the foot of the mountain of God.
We heard the thunder of his coming,

saw the flashes of his glory,
heard the sound of his voice,
and caught his trumpet blast
upon the desert air.

Yet we were kept apart,
as if we were not worthy to approach,
as if God were for grown-ups,
and only Moses was mature enough
for his grandeur and his liking.
As if we were not good enough.

So Moses climbed alone
to where the bounds of heaven began,
and stepped across the shining line
into the arms of the divine.
God's pupil, God's companion,
God's friend, God's lover he became.

Once, only once, he took his brother with him,
and his brother's sons,
and seventy men gnarled with wisdom,
and they put their feet under God's table,
and ate his meat and drank his wine,
and took their fill of visions.

But we were left to kick our heels
and pace our tents
and eat our manna and be thankful.
We found this God beyond us,
and ourselves left out.
We behaved accordingly.

⁊⁊

And now once more we find ourselves in a deserted
place.
This time we have edged around the sea.
We did not need its splitting to get here,
yet not because it's safer now.
The Egyptians are on both sides of the water.
A miracle will not save us this time,

for they have entered on our promised land,
They have changed their name to Romans, but the
cruelty is familiar.
Our women are still raped, our children killed,
whole villages up in smoke,
for casting sling-stones at the one they call high Emperor.
Goliath is better prepared these days.

And we have come to this deserted place to get away
from it all,
away from the tramping soldiers,
away from those who drive us into poverty and
then despise us for it,
who block our roads, demolish our homes,
uproot our vineyards, and turn our ancient lands
into their settlements,
and fill our eyes with stinking tears, and crush us
with their tanks.

We have nothing in our hands now,
nothing we could rescue.
We do not know where the next meal will come from.
For we have nothing in our hands,
no gold to turn into a calf,
no means to make our merriment.

Will God keep us at arm's length again,
    too keen to hide his mystery,
    too protective of his glory?
        Our hands are empty.
        Will he deny us,
            and we him?

∽

'I have no meat or wine to give you.
I have nowhere to lay my head.
They have driven me out, like you.
Fish and bread will have to do for now.
But I will give you more than you can eat,
and fill twelve baskets with the scraps.

'For you will eat the bread of love,
and I will wrap your food in blessing,
and show you tastes of heaven.
And in this desert place
I will once more plant Eden,
and give you all its fruit.

'You are too tired to climb to heaven, as
    Moses did,
your feet too sore,
your backs too bent and scarred.
So I will walk among you,
and wait upon you all,
as always is my wont.

'And I will wash your feet,
and rub your backs,
and put the spring back in your step,

and raise your heads,
and crown you with fine mercy,
all that heaven can muster!

'And if they ask you
where you've been,
and who you've spoken with,
then tell them you've been feasting with
    your God,
and fill their ears
with his bright tales and merry laugh.

'One day, perhaps,
they will put down their arms
and sit with us and cry and laugh.
And I will serve them too,
and wash their feet.
For they have marched through too
    much blood.'

AND MOSES REPLIED

*I have taken great liberties in this piece. It is not fair to Moses.
(I have done him greater justice, perhaps, in the story called 'The
Hermit', which you will find earlier in this book.) And yet it is
true to the anger of his remarkable prayers in Exodus 5.22–23
and Numbers 11.11–15, and to the bitterness and occasional
sarcasm of prayer elsewhere in the Old Testament (think for a
moment of Psalm 88, or of Job shaking his fist at God in the
poetic section of that book). It reminds us, also, of the horror of
the story of the Burning Bush in Exodus 3—4, where, so some
rabbinic commentators tell us, Moses looks into the furnace of
Egypt and sees his people caught in the flames. It attempts to
avoid being romantic about the impact of suffering or oppression
upon people and their faith. And it alerts us to just how radical
and demanding are the words of the Beatitudes of Matthew 5.*

He had seen. Seen God, and seen his people in the furnace of
Egypt. God had opened the door a crack for him, and shown
him the flames. He had been beaten back by the heat. He had
fallen to the desert ground, while the flames licked at the
branches of the bush and turned them red as blood.

He had protested. He had protested, but God's ears had been
stopped, too full of the cries of his people across the other side
of the Red Sea. He had protested until the flames of the bush
no longer burned silently, but filled the desert with their roar.

In the end God had given him no choice. And so he had
returned. He had entered the furnace. For all their roaring, the
flames of the bush at the mountain of God had not destroyed
him, nor consumed at all. The flames of the furnace were different, containing no miracle.

So he took off his sandals once again, and laid them on the soil of Egypt, and spread his hands before God. A darkness fell thick upon the land, and silence as large as the universe. Words fell from heaven, soft as manna upon a wilderness floor.

> Blessed are the poor in spirit, for theirs is the kingdom
> of heaven.
> Blessed are those who mourn, for they will be
> comforted.
> Blessed are the meek, for they will inherit the earth.
> Blessed are the pure in heart, for they shall see God.

And Moses replied, 'Thank God you're Almighty, God! Because I can't see how all that could happen if you weren't! So we're in for a bit of fun, now are we? Tables turned and all that. As you say, the meek inheriting the earth. In fact, we don't need the whole earth. Egypt and Palestine will do nicely.'

His head was suddenly bursting with ideas. 'How about turning all their water to blood, and their light into darkness, and bringing on a few frogs and gnats and flies and locusts, and throwing around some hail and animal pestilence, and boils for good measure? . . . and if that doesn't do the trick, then how about killing all their first-born, and burning Egypt to ash with grief? . . . and we can have a jolly party and dress ourselves in their finery and dance upon their graves till we fall over with their liquor . . . then we won't be poor in spirit anymore, we'll be up to our eyeballs with the stuff, and our days of mourning will be over for good, and we won't have to be meek any longer . . . and we'll conga our way to your holy mountain and see you face to face, and you will be our God and we will be your people, for ever and ever . . . and if they shake themselves free from their grief in time and rise up from their calamities and come chasing after us, then you can split the Red Sea in two, just like you sliced the Monster of Chaos at the Creation of the World, and you can lead us all across safely, like a shepherd leading his sheep, even the children, even the bruised and the battered, even the tortured and the broken, even the very frail and the old-as-Methuselahs, even the women carrying children and nearing their time, even the doubting Jacobs . . . and when we're all across, you can let the waters loose, like you did at the Flood, and they'll crash down on the Egyptians and their horses and their clattering chariots and their pharaoh riding as high as a god, and we'll watch it all and sing a fine song as their bloated bodies come rocking towards the shore? How about *that*, Almighty God?

The darkness grew thicker still, and the silence yet more pressing. For a second time words fell into the palms of Moses' hands:

> Blessed are the merciful, for they will receive mercy.
> Blessed are the peacemakers, for they will be called
> the children of God.

Moses could not stand their gentleness. 'It is not the time for our mercy!' he cried. 'It is high time we *received* some! We're in no position to give any, and won't be till you've bashed the Egyptians to pieces! Mercy is for the powerful and the strong. We have no power at all. Why else do you think we need you to fling yours around? We are weak as water. Why else do we need you to turn our water into wine? It's up to the Egyptians to show us some mercy, and if they won't, then it's up to you to show them none. And as for peacemaking! How do you suppose we're going to do that? How can we negotiate with the pharaoh? He's a thug, and you know it. His people are hysterical. They can't wait for his next orders. How do you think we can make an ounce of peace? Peacemaking is for the Egyptians to get on with. We'd like some peace from them!

'It's alright for you, God! You don't get hurt. Yours is the

greatness, the power, the glory, the splendour, and the majesty.
Everything in heaven and on earth is yours. You can afford to
be merciful. You can make any peace you choose. You don't get
hurt. Hell is not for you! Its flames can't reach across the gulf
to your precious heaven, or lick around your throne!'

The words from heaven came a third time and lay themselves at Moses' feet:

> Blessed are the merciful, for they will receive mercy.
> Blessed are the peacemakers, for they will be called
>   children of God.

Moses stamped them into the ground, turned on his heel and
walked away. Behind him the nails twisted in God's hands and
feet, and the desert thorns bit deep into his forehead.

THE FOOT-WASHING

*I first preached this piece in Chester Cathedral on a Maundy
Thursday. The service included the washing of the feet of some
members of the congregation, and I got into slight trouble with
my colleagues for using too much soap. Since then we have not
used soap at all. The little story in John 13.1–5 of Jesus washing
his disciples' feet is one of those that seems to capture the essence
of his life and work. Strictly speaking, it is not a part of the
passion narrative in John, the story of Jesus' arrest, trials and
crucifixion. Yet we do well to recall it as we set out for Golgotha.*

*I have given special prominence in this piece to the anointing
of Jesus by an unnamed woman in Mark 14.3–9, or Matthew
26.6–13. In John the woman who performs the deed is given a
name, Mary of Bethany. But in that Gospel the anointing is
again detached from the passion narrative, whereas Mark's and
Matthew's versions are not.*

*Nearer the end of the piece are two references to the book of
Genesis, the first to the story of God and Sarah entertaining
God in Genesis 18, the second to the first part of the Garden
of Eden story in Genesis 2.*

From here there is no going back.
We are drawn inexorably to Golgotha.
A few moments and we will be there,
pulled by our annual fascination with this
    man's death,
driven by our longing for salvation,
the need to know we are saved, safe,
and loved to the bitter end.

A few moments and Jesus will be there also,
for the Son of God will be strung up high,
pinned tight for all to see.

But first some stories must be told,
a few things must be done.
And we must watch and listen,
and let God touch our souls.

First the Son of God must come near to
      breaking point
among the shining olives of Gethsemane.

First he must be embraced and kissed by an
      old comrade
(an expensive kiss – thirty pieces of silver).

First he must be arrested,
taken for trial,
thrown into the deep end of men's power games,
kicked between a mob baying for crucifixion,
clever men trying to keep their hands clean,
and soldiers using him as their prey
for their own beloved brand of blood sport.

First he must be denied
by another friend,
once, twice, three times,
and a cock must crow.

First he must be abandoned by all
but a few women
and – alone in John –
the disciple who means so much.

Before that an unnamed woman
must anoint him Messiah
in the house of Simon the leper.
She must do what the high priest should have
    done long ago.
A leper's house in Bethany must serve
for the anointing of the Son of God,
when only the fine, grand temple in Jerusalem
was good enough for the rest of David's kings.

That unnamed woman
must prepare the Son of God
for his enthronement.
She will do her job well.
She will pour the perfume of her love all over
    his head.

The soldiers will see to the crowning
and the placing on the throne.
They too will do their job well,
alas.

But first of all in John
the Son of God must teach his friends a parable.
He must take off the clothes of a rabbi
and put on the towel of a disciple,
kneel beside a bowl of water,
and wash feet clean from the world's dirt,
make them tingle, bring a shine to the skin.

To wash a rabbi's feet is an act of love.
To wash disciples' feet
is to set love free from all convention
and let it roam the whole wide world.

When God came in disguise to ancient Abraham,
with two companions trailing behind them the
    light of heaven
and all the hope Sarah and Abraham longed for,
Abraham did not wash his feet.
'Let a little water be fetched,' he said,
'And wash your feet.'
Those were all the courtesies
entertaining God unawares
demanded then.

But now the Son of God does the washing.
Such are the courtesies of Golgotha;
such is the etiquette of heaven.

Jesus is not play-acting here.
This particular parable is for real,
like the pilgrimage to Golgotha along the
    Via Dolorosa
and the pain at that journey's end.

There is no pretending here.
God had a towel round his waist
when he made the world;
a potter's apron tied around him
when he knelt in Eden
to puff the life into the first human being;
a surgeon's gown,
when he took that creature's side and made
    a woman.

He has never lorded it over us,
and never will.

He always treats us like royalty.
Go to Golgotha and we will see.

11 THE SILENCE OF THE CROSS

Only one of the friends and companions of Jesus is named in all four Gospels as being present at Jesus' crucifixion, and that is Mary of Magdala. In Matthew, Mark and Luke she is also among the first to discover the resurrection, and in John is the first to encounter the risen Jesus himself. Mark, at 15.41, tells us she had 'followed and provided for' Jesus when he was in Galilee, and Luke speaks of that, also, and adds that Jesus had freed her from the grip of 'seven demons' (Luke 8.1–3). How we interpret those 'seven demons' is left up to us, though clearly Luke means us to imagine a catastrophe of some kind which was utterly consuming her. I have imagined not an illness, but a terrible act of abuse such as many women of Mary's time and place must have suffered under Roman occupation, and which, alas, far too many women of our own day have been subjected to in time of war.

Towards the end of this piece I make particular reference to the story of Mary's meeting with the risen Jesus in John 20.11–18. The phrase I use earlier of 'life like a watered garden' is from Jeremiah 31.12.

'It was the silence I could not bear. Behind all the shouting, behind the abuse and pain, a fearful silence. I had to look on from a distance, as if watching a silent film.

'The soldiers didn't help. I don't just mean their bullying, their lewd comments and racism, their shoving us about, touching us up, keeping us apart. I'd had dealings with soldiers before. You couldn't avoid dealings with soldiers, either in Jerusalem, or in Galilee, or in Magdala. I'd been raped by soldiers in Magdala, my mother and my two sisters, too. A common enough experience, of course. Plenty of other families, in plenty of other towns and villages. But that experience was mine, and my mother's and my sisters', too. I saw them rape my mother and sisters. They ordered me to watch. Then it was my turn. It still happens, of course.

'I thought I'd never recover. I thought I was dirty and would never be clean again. I thought I was trash that any man would despise. I said to myself, 'No man will marry me now.' We drowned in our shame, all four of us. There was no air for us to breathe; our lungs were choked with filth.

'My mother and sisters caught some terrible sickness from it, and died, one by one. That's when I knew what it was to be alive and dead at the same time. I retreated into silence and curled up inside it, wishing death would come to me too, knowing I was already dead inside, rotting to a stench.

'And that's when he arrived in Magdala and led me through to resurrection! He didn't bring me back to life. He led me through my death to a life beyond that I could never have dreamed of, even before the soldiers came – 'life like a watered garden', as one of our prophets put it. And it was God's garden, and mine also, and – he showed me this, though at first I didn't want to look – a garden for the soldiers who had burst into our house that day, a place waiting for them, where they might with us enjoy God's company.

'That's what I mean, he didn't just bring me back to life. He gave me courage, a quite new dignity, and the strength to love my enemies.

'Yet there, on Golgotha, that strength deserted me. It wasn't just the soldiers. They had taken away my lord, my friend, and I could see only too well where they had laid him!

'I fled back to my old silence and tried to twist myself again into its little space. Once more I longed for death to come: to my friend, to bring an end to his long agonies; to me, because my pain also was past enduring. Once more I caught the stench of death inside me.

'Yet there was a silence greater than mine. I mean the silence of heaven. That was the silence I could not bear.

'My friend said something from the cross. But it was like watching a silent film and I cannot lip read. I don't know what he said. All I know is this: I went to his tomb when the sabbath was over, in the heavy silence of the dawn, shrouded tight in my despair, my ears full of the emptiness of heaven . . . and I found myself in a garden that shone with memories of him, memories of his meeting me at Magdala, memories of that love in Galilee, memories of resurrection! And then my silences were broken once for all by a single word, my name, "Mary!" He gave me the courage then, the dignity and the pride, the strength to love even his enemies.

'Heaven has not been silent since, nor ever can be. I, Mary of Magdala, am twice risen from the dead! Come with me and I will show you what forgiveness means and teach you all its ways. They are beyond belief.'

12   'IT IS FINISHED'

The quotation with which this piece begins is a line from T. S. Eliot's 'Four Quartets'. My subject is the crucifixion of Jesus, and I have borrowed the title from the passion narrative of John 19.30.

'Human kind,' the poet said, 'cannot bear very much
    reality.'
Yet things catch up on us, of course,
rise from troubled depths to trouble us;
the mist of our pretence clears,
and moments come too hard and sharp
when we neglect to fool ourselves.

Then we need a safe place,
where we will not be judged,
but understood.
We do not need another's scorn;
we need compassion.
When truth rises up
and breaks the surface of our pretending,
we do not need our failings or our failures
pointed out and underlined.
We need a reminder of our worth,
a new impression of our dignity,
so we can laugh at ourselves
with laughter that is merry and without mockery.

Too many of us believe we cannot attain even to
     mediocrity,
for we are measured by what we have achieved,
and told our very worth depends on it.
The air sits heavy with our disappointment.

Bereavement and grief or the end of relationship
knock the stuffing out of us.
The guilt so often left behind,
the anxiety, the emptiness,
the noiseless house to return to,
the silent evenings,
the having no-one now to tell about our day,
no-one to share our fears,
the home that is no longer quite itself,
these can sap our confidence,
seek to undermine our worth.

Persistent pain or chronic fear can do the same,
and loneliness, also.
Being other people's outcasts,
living perpetually on the edge of things,
being not loved for all we are worth,
feeling we are not loved at all,
these most surely do it,
persuade us we count for little,
or nothing.

Yet that is a lie!
It is not true,
not true,
not true!

༄

See here,
here on this cross,
is a man in pain.
Here is a man alone.
Here is a man who faced arrest
among the black olives of Gethsemane
and almost broke apart with fear.
Here is a man cast out,
taken outside the walls for execution,
lest he contaminate the holy city by his dying.
Here is a man overcome by loss,
drowning in the last moment of his agony,
in the silence of God.
And what in all this had he achieved?

This man carried the humanity of us all,
and still bears its load.

And this man shows us God.

See here,
here on this cross,
we see God outcast,
God in pain,
God unloved,
God alone,
God sorely grieved.

Yet here is God with arms stretched wide for
      our embrace;
here fall heaven's tears of love;
here we catch the beating of God's heart;
here is God's generosity displayed
and here his victory unfurled!

For God is not defeated here.
Love wins this day,
and must win every day.
Nothing can confound the Love of God,
nothing deflect it from its course,
or stem its flow.

So here,
in the shadow of this cross,
we are not alone;
here our grief and pain are understood, shared,
    cherished;
here is healing for our torn souls;
here, where terror might seem to hold such sway,
we have no cause to fear;
here we are loved,
loved still more,
loved eternally
with a Love that has no flaw,
that will not let us down,
that is as large and larger than the universe,
as bright as a kingfisher's back in the summer's sun,
as strong and relentless as the crash of the sea.

We are worth something here!
We are worth everything here!
Let us care for one another.

The stories of the Ascension of Christ are to be found at the very end of Luke's Gospel, at 24.50–53, and at the start of the Acts of the Apostles, at 1.6–11.

'What can this mean,
this Ascension?
Is it cause for celebration,
or for grief?
Is it triumph,
or parting?
So much hangs on the answer.
The stories tell of both.
They speak of parting,
disappearance,
of Christ going away
to where we cannot follow –
not till death brings
our own resurrection and ascension.
Yet they also speak of triumph,
of glory,
exaltation,
heaven all a-ring with alleluias.
Which of these is of the truth?'

'Both of them, my friend.
The stories can be trusted.
Ascension is both triumph and parting,
two faces of the same,
a time for sorrow and for joy.

We speak of the Cross
as the place of Christ's triumph,
and so it was.
But triumph then
was not without its fearsome ambiguity.
How can we call such brutality
as was there on Golgotha,
such pain and fighting for breath,
such inevitable dying,
such utter loneliness,
where even God himself
seemed to hide for very fear,
how can we call that triumph,
and say no more?
It was, of course, a victory
for reconciliation,
for generosity,
for humility,
for integrity,
for courage,
for love,
for meekness strong as steel,
for all that is good.
Of course it was.
Resurrection taught us that,
and ring out alleluias for it!
But we cannot leave it there.
We cannot leave God there.
Let Christ be put aloft
in heavenly double-decker bus!
Let him be paraded
through the streets of the heavenly Jerusalem,
holding up the cross for all to see!
Let him be deafened

by the cheers of angels!
Let God be reunited,
instead of torn to pieces!
Let Christ feel the warmth again
of the divine embrace!
For God's sake let him know
God had not deserted him!
Let him get the mockery of the soldiers
and the fears of the priests
out of his head!
Let him know love,
let him be fair bathed in it!
Let him drink the wine of heaven,
instead of the vinegar of Golgotha!
Let him take his place once more
in the dance and the laughter
of the Trinity!
Oh yes,
let that be,
let that be!

'And let us catch the echoes
of all this celebrating,
and have a chance
to throw our own caps in the air!
Let all manner of things,
all manner of things be well,
and let us know,
deep in the depths of our souls,
that that is so.
Let us glimpse,
behind the ambiguity
of this familiar world,
another realm,

where God is love,
and God is loved,
and that is all there is.
No caveats,
no qualifications,
no yes but's.
God is love,
God is loved,
and that is all there is.

'This familiar world of ours
is too full of caveats,
and qualifications,
of yes but's,
and worse.
Even on heady days,
when hope runs high,
we know it will not all last.
God will be denied again;
we will deny God again,
and fail once more
to come to terms with an eternal love
that is so utterly unencumbered with strings,
and given with such wild, unstinting prodigality.
All is not well here,
nor, while we are around,
will ever be.

'God is absent here,
as much as God is present,
or that is how it feels.
For us it is one
of the world's enduring realities.
We face it every day.

'Preachers will tell you
that Ascension Day
is not about Christ's going away
and leaving us behind.
Yet that is how the ancient story goes,
and those the terms in which it speaks.
And for us,
in this place,
it is part of the truth of it,
part of our truth,
and part of God's, also.
God does not belong here,
though he made his home here,
long before Bethlehem,
long before the earth was marked
by any human print.
God does not belong here,
because we have refused to make him welcome.
It is as simple as that,
and as devastating.
So God belongs in heaven,
and must return there,
while we are left behind,
for the moment,
till our own resurrection and ascension,
till our own reunion,
with ourselves,
with one another,
with creation,
with God.
Till that moment comes
we are left behind
to do God's work,
give him some co-operation,

hang out the bunting,
put up the balloons,
put on the kettle,
and bid him welcome.

'For, of course, God does belong here, too.
This is God's home,
as much as heaven.
He has been here
before we were a twinkle in his eye.
This is God's home,
this *is* God's home,
and we must set about as best we can,
and make him welcome.'

This is a story about two charcoal fires, the one in John 18.15–18, 25–27, beside which Peter denies Jesus, and the other in John 21.4–17, where the risen and ascended Christ appears to Peter and others of the disciples on the shore of the Sea of Galilee. I make reference also to many other passages in the Gospels, among them Mark 8.27–33, where Peter declares Jesus Messiah but fails to come to terms with his response, and the story of Jesus washing his disciples' feet in John 13.1–11, and to the description in all four Gospels of Mary of Magdala as a witness to the crucifixion.

   Mention of the Sea of Galilee immediately brings to my mind the times I have spent there on pilgrimage. I have woven some of my memories into the fabric of the piece.

'It was early. The sun was still hidden behind the Golan hills, the churches of the holy sites were not yet open, and the buses full of pilgrims were not yet on the road. The Sea of Galilee – or the Sea of Kingfishers as I call it, there are so many of them there – lay very quiet. Only the smallest of waves ruffled the shoreline. White egrets flew silently from their roosts, and the first kingfishers began diving for their fish, disturbing the dawn with small splashes, emerging with little fish shining in their bills. The air shone with unusual clarity. In the far distance the high snows of Mount Hermon turned pink in the new sun.

'We had gone back to our fishing. We were trying to forget. Turn the clock back and go back to the beginning. Go back to Galilee, to familiar waters, to the old boats and the old ways. As if nothing had occurred. Push out the boats, cast the nets, haul them in, as if nothing had happened.

'But, of course, it had. There was no pretending. You cannot go back to the beginning, because when you get there you find it has changed from when you started out. You cannot undo the past. You cannot go back to a past you would prefer to remember, as if the in-between, the things which you long to forget, had never been. Escape is not that easy, nor that possible.

'Of course, there were things in-between we wanted to remember. Jesus himself for one, and his jokes, and the parties we had into the small hours, and his strange, disturbing stories and the words he came out with, and his uncanny knack of reaching the heart of everyone he met, and the way he turned things upside-down, and his getting so angry with those who thought religion was more important than people, and the friendships he created. All that we wanted to remember. But not the journey to Jerusalem and the soldiers. Not the pleading with him to be more careful. Not the telling him to stop being so stupid. Not the, who did he think he was, the bloody Messiah? and him reminding me that that was precisely what I'd said he was just a moment before. I didn't want to remember that. Nor Herod and Pilate. Nor the pretence of a trial, and the sham of another, and his yells as he was being beaten. Nor the courtyard of the high priest's house and the charcoal fire. I didn't want to remember that. God! I didn't want to remember that.

'Yet I kept on remembering. Over and over again. How cold it was that night of the trial. How glad I was of the fire. How I was sitting there all in a daze, thinking I was safe, when that wretched slave-girl recognized me. "Hey, you were with him!" she shouted. She said it again later. Told everyone she did, the interfering little . . . as I used to call her. Then the others heard my northern accent and started joining in, and before I knew it the dawn came and the cock crowed, just as he'd said it would. I broke down then. No more bravado. I got the hell out of it. I missed the crucifixion. So did the others. Except Mary of Magdala. She'd always had a rare courage, had Mary of Magdala, ever since he'd cured her of her terrible illness. After that she'd never cared about anyone else. The soldiers would have had to kill her to keep her away.

'But I wasn't there. I'd done a runner. I'd failed. I'd let him down. Three times I'd said I didn't even know who he was. And I wasn't there when he died. I'd funked it. I'd gone away to hide in a corner and cry my eyes out. Mary had been made of sterner stuff, and had a deeper love for him than I did. When it came to it I didn't love him enough. It was as simple as that.

'So there we were, out fishing on the Sea of Galilee, pretending we were back where we began. We were fools! For God's sake, we were back where it had all started with *him*! The place was full of him. You could smell him in the air. His voice was in the cries of the birds. The shore was marked all over by his steps. Even the waters of the lake seemed to have his stamp upon them. And this time there was no escape, no doing a runner, no hiding in a corner.

'Another charcoal fire was burning on the shore, like the one in the courtyard of the high priest's house. And breakfast turned into a eucharist. In a few hours' time the busloads of pilgrims would be scattering themselves beside the shore, huddling round their bread and wine. We were there already, with his bread and our fish.

'Three times he asked me if I loved him. Three times he gave me the chance to replace denial with love. Three times I took that chance. And three times he called me shepherd of his sheep. Do you know what shepherd means? Long before David and Solomon, long before our ancestors came to this land, kings called themselves "shepherds" of their people. Jesus was calling me king, and that breakfast of bread and fish was my coronation banquet!

'But what sort of king should I be? I didn't have to ask that.

I just had to remember how he had exercised his royalty, with a towel round his waist, and at the last, when they'd got round to his enthronement, a cross for a throne.

'I have hurt him more times than three since then. I'm only human, after all, not the saint of your stained-glass windows. But I have found the love for him that Mary of Magdala always had, and the strength and the courage that goes with it. How could I not love him, when he took the script of my denial and burned it to ashes in a charcoal fire, and filled the air of Galilee with talk of love, and then placed a crown on my head? "You look ridiculous!" he cried then, and our laughter was so loud, a group of early pilgrims turned in our direction and scowled at us for disturbing their devotions. "But then," he added more quietly, "I too looked ridiculous on that cross, me, the king of the Jews, and the very Son of God. Wear your crown with courage, my old friend. And remember, the love is mutual."

'I have not forgotten.'

The beginning of this piece refers to legends about St Thomas which are hugely important to Christians in some parts of the world, but little known in Britain. From them I turn to the famous story about Thomas in John 20.24–29. At that stage I might seem to indulge in some special pleading on Thomas's behalf. In truth I am trying to be fair to the Thomas that John portrays, and to give due weight to the great climax of the passage (one might almost say the climax of John's entire Gospel), Thomas's exclamation in 20.28, 'My Lord and my God!'

'I'm a one-story man, except in India, where they'll tell you I was the first to come to their land and teach about Jesus of Nazareth. Ask the Christians of Mylapore, near Madras. They'll speak of my martyrdom and my burial there. But they won't be able to show you my bones. They say they were taken to Edessa in the fourth century, in Syria, and from there to Ortona, wherever that is. I don't know where I am any more!'

Thomas laughed. 'Where was I? Ah, yes, a one-story man. Except in Parthia (part of what you call Iran, I believe). They say I brought the gospel there, too, and – do you know what? – this will surprise you – surprised me when I first heard it, and would have surprised my old Mum, as well, bless her – who do you think my twin was, according to the Christians in that part of the world, around Iran and such? Because I was a twin, of course. *They* say my twin brother was Jesus himself! Goes back a long way apparently, that idea. If you want to know, by the way, my real twin was called Rachel.

'Anyway, you don't hold with all that stuff. As far as you're concerned, I'm a one-story man, a one-word man, in fact. I'm doubting Thomas, that's who I am. Doubt personified. The embodiment, the very epitome of doubt. End of story. End of me. And doubt, of course, is wrong, and you, of course, don't have a single doubt in your heads. You let me do all the doubting for you and get the ticking-off, while you hide behind me and pretend your belief is as firm as a rock.

'Read on, my friends, read on, just three verses later in that story you think you know so well. Three verses later, there I am saying, "My Lord and my God!" Does that sound like doubt to you? It doesn't sound like it to me. I'm the first person in John's story of Jesus to come out with those words. The whole of his story leads up to them. "My Lord and my God." At last someone has seen the truth and spoken it clearly. Everything that has gone before leads to that moment. And I provide it. I say the words. With my own lips. Me, your very own Doubting Thomas!

'But you still look down on me, don't you, from your spiritual high ground. *You* haven't placed your finger on the risen Christ. You haven't reached out your hand and put it in his side. And yet you still believe. Not like me. I had to have proof.

'But what sort of proof do you think I had? Do you really think I touched him with my bare hands? Do you really think he could be touched at all like that? I tell you, I was face to face with my God! Huddled with the others in that house, waiting for the Romans to come and arrest us at any moment, I found myself in the presence of God, and knew him for the first time.

'I had known him all along, of course, ever since I'd met him in Galilee. But at that moment I saw for the first time who he was. And I knew then Pilate hadn't broken him, after all. I knew it was true, what they said about his death being his finest hour. His crucifixion was his triumph, God's triumph, and victory for that ancient love of God that passes all our understandings.

'Do you think I *touched God*? Look at my new grandson here, nearly new-born. You can hold him and hear him, and smell him at times, too. You can tell me his name. But can you put your finger on who he is? Can you grasp his small mystery? Can you show it to me in your hand and say, "Here it is"? Of course not. It's too large for you, altogether. All the words in all the world cannot tell his truth. It's already far too extraordinary.

'So if my little grandson flummoxes you, if he is so far beyond your reach, what do you think it was like for me when I came to my senses and found myself in the very presence of God, in his holy of holies, so to speak, where I thought only the high priest went once a year? Do you really think I could place my hand upon my God? Of course not.

'*He* put his hand on *me*! Or rather, he put his arms round me. I still bear the marks of his hands upon my back. I shall never forget that embrace. It is what I mean by resurrection.

'Come now. Don't look so serious! His embrace was not, is not, just for me. See, my grandson carries the marks of it, too! If you haven't yet noticed them on yourself, then look at him!

'Oh, and no more of this "doubting Thomas" stuff. Alright?'

This is perhaps the most straightforward piece in the collection, and the one in which I have used my imagination the least. All the things which God 'shows' Thomas are based on incidents which have actually taken place, some of them repeatedly. I could, of course, have chosen worse.

There was a knock on God's door, and Thomas came in. 'You look worried, Thomas, my friend,' God said. 'Bothered about your doubts again?'

'Yes, God.'

'But I thought we had settled all that.'

'Yes, we had.'

'Well then?'

'They tell me, they still tell me that doubt is a sin.'

'No doubt they are entirely sure of that.'

'Oh yes.'

God flushed with anger. 'Your doubt a sin! I tell you, I am terrified of their certainty! Their faith is a baseball bat, and every time they catch you in one of their dark alleys, they beat you about the head with it. They want to knock the sense out of you. They want to knock the Thomas out of you, and turn you into one of them. It's all about power, their power, though they say it's about mine. Come and sit down, and I will give you something for your poor head.'

God's room, with its scent of the flowers of Galilee, always reassured Thomas. God always reassured Thomas.

God soothed Thomas's wounds. 'You remember the battering I had,' God said. 'That was all about power, too.'

When the work was done, and Thomas was healed once

more, God got up suddenly and said, 'Come with me. I want to show you a few things.'

God took Thomas to an open space outside a prison. It was approaching midnight. Inside a man was being strapped tight to an ugly black contraption, ready for the injections that would kill him. He had been on death row for ten years. High on drugs he had once murdered an old woman. Now, as the moment of his own death approached, a group of men and woman outside waved placards and Bibles and bawled the vengeance of their god.

God took Thomas to an abortion clinic. A doctor emerged from the front door and was hustled into a car by two body-guards, as in the name of God a crowd hurled their abuse. 'Hitler!' they shouted, 'Murderer! Baby killer!'

'They'll be shouting "Crucify him!" next,' God murmured.

God took Thomas to the city he knew all too well, to Jerusalem, showed him the Jewish settlers strolling through the streets with their machine guns slung casually over their shoulders, stood silently with him as they shouted, 'This is *our* land! God gave it to our ancestors, to Abraham, Isaac, and Jacob, and to no-one else. He did not give it to Ishmael. He gave it to us!'

God took Thomas a bus ride away to the house of an archaeologist in a suburb of the city. The telephone rang. The caller did not identify himself. 'You are digging in the area of the Temple Mount,' the voice said. 'I have seen you and your people there. You are digging up the bones of our ancestors. You are defiling holy ground. The rabbis have put a curse on you all. You will get cancer and die. That will put a stop to your digging!' The telephone went dead.

God took Thomas to a church where a preacher of very long and very loud sermons was denouncing 'the papists' yet again. The congregation was loving it.

God took Thomas to a second church, where another

preacher was busy pouring scorn on other religions. 'If you have a statue of the Buddha, or a copy of the Koran in your home, bin them!' he was saying, and hundreds and hundreds were hanging on his every word.

'Would he say that to a Buddhist or a Muslim?' Thomas asked. 'Would he say that to their face?'

'I don't know,' God replied. 'He has hardly met any, nor have the people listening to him.'

Thomas turned away. 'I have seen enough,' he said.

'So have I,' said God. 'You see now why I prefer your doubts, Thomas,' she added.

17 THE RAVEN-BLACK SPIRIT OF GOD

In the stories in the Gospels of the baptism of Jesus the Spirit of God is compared to a dove. In this piece I have compared it to a raven. I do not mean to be perverse. It is just that ravens, or one particular pair of ravens, have come to mean a great deal to me. Since 1996 a pair has nested, quite remarkably, right in the centre of Chester, and for most of those years on the tower of the Cathedral, with the nest in full view of my study window. I have celebrated the Eucharist of an early morning surrounded by a large silence broken only by the faint honking of ravens. I have seen the adults displaying, or weaving the basket of their nest. I have looked through my telescope, set up in my study window, at the full-grown young flexing their wings. One year I caught the moment when one of the young took its first flight. They are extraordinary birds, and still my heart leaps every time I see them, or hear them call. They show me something of God.

In this story I have put them back into the wilder environment of mountain and cliff, with which we normally associate ravens in this country, and from which the parents of the Chester ravens probably came.

'Look! There she flies! I knew we would find her here.'

We were sitting on a wild April mountainside, with a small stream, bursting with spring rains, rushing just beyond our feet. A cold wind blew, and we were glad of the shelter of the rock at our backs.

'Where?' I asked.

My companion pointed high above the steep crag that faced us. A bird, or so it seemed, was tumbling in the wind, playing with its soaring, swirling currents. She had all the freedom of the air and more. It was as if she gave the sky its freedom, and so indeed she did. For at the beginning, when the world was made, she had untied the sky from the earth's weight, to let it float high and wide, a playground for the angels and herself, for divine somersaults and cartwheels.

She flew above us now, the raven-black Spirit of God, turned on her back for a second, for the sheer fun of it, and gave us a soft call of recognition. She was black from the point of her bill to the end of her tail, and from tip to tip of her long wings. Even her eye was black. Yet the sheen in her feathers and the glint in her eye threw off the sunlight and turned her to silver and to gold.

My friend had long kept this God company. He had watched as she built her nest high on the crag, weaving together twigs snapped off the trees in the dark valley below, binding them one to another, till they could withstand the fiercest gales that came in from a winter's sea. He had seen her weaving a circlet of the finest willow, to crown the lip of the round nest-bowl. He had spied her flying in with beakfuls of moss taken from the trees of Eden for the nest's lining, strips of bark from the branches of the Tree of Life, small clumps of wool taken from the fences where the Scapegoat had been rubbing itself against the itch of others' guilt. In the middle of a pile of twigs that was itself a work of divine engineering, the nest-bowl she made with feet and bill became a masterpiece of heaven's art. The angels lost themselves in admiration, though the Spirit of God had not built the nest for their applause, but as a place of life. How could it be otherwise with the Spirit of God?

So the eggs were laid, one the blue of a morning sky, the others the green of leaves in bud, splashed with chocolate brown. For days on end the winds blew, and the mountain rains fell as if trying to wash the cliff away, but God's patience kept the eggs warm and the life within them, also. She held them against her brood-patch, saved them by her touch and by the pulsing heat of her blood. (Without the brood-patch of the Spirit of God there would be no life at all. It is how things first came to be, and how they are sustained. The warmth of God's drenched body keeps us all from the cold.)

'And from the rain,' I said.

The wind had got up and the first spots already teared our faces. Soon it was coming at us horizontally, battering our cheeks, commanding us to withdraw. Unable to tear ourselves away, we stood our ground, while high above us the raven-shining Spirit of God did not flinch either. The eggs had hatched, but beneath her wings, half spread to shelter them, the young did not feel a drop of rain, nor the blows of the gale, though their mother's body sometimes rocked with its violence. And when, all of a sudden, the rain stopped and the wind disappeared to fan the rays of the sun, and stoking heat attacked the crag with even greater force than had the storm, then her panting wings shielded them still. As they had survived because of the warmth of her body, so now they lived through the cool of her intimacy.

Through storm and heat, through frosty nights, dense mountain mist and searing afternoons the young continued to grow beneath her feathers, until they were too large for the nest. Now they spent their time not in, but on the nest, clambering over one another, flexing their wing muscles, playing at nest-building by rearranging the smaller twigs or clumps of Scapegoat's wool.

My companion and I waited for the day when the first of them would fly. It would not be long coming. We watched her, the Mother God, the raven-winged Spirit of God, as she flew towards the nest as if again to feed her young. This time, at this momentous hour, she circled several times before coming in, as if to put ideas in their heads. As she reached the nest, bills were opened wide to receive her food (like hands stretched out at altar rail, but with greater urgency and much more noise). She pushed food down the first bill she came to, but the second was suddenly refused. Instead she spread her wings and let the breeze lift her, and, as she did so, the second bird jumped lightly off the twigs, arched its wings and floated with her high above our heads. Together, their wing-tips almost touching, they crossed the heavens, while we chorused our delight. Over the next few days we watched as, one by one, the Spirit of God gave her young the high freedom of the air.

When the last had gone and the nest was empty, I asked, 'Are we too old then for the comfort of God's nest and the warmth of her brood-patch? Must we be for ever on the wing, if we are to stay with her?'

'For the most part, yes,' my friend replied. 'Yet God has no territory to defend. She does not claim the mountain for herself, nor drive her young away. She flies with us, if we will let her, and sometimes, if the gale is too fierce or the cold bites too deep, then she lets us find again her shelter in the round nest-bowl. We live for ever within the circle of her wings. She will never desert us, nor leave us empty, undefended.'

A faint, repeated cronking filled our ears, and looking up we saw her very high above us, twisting, swooping, tumbling, hurling herself about the sky with gay, divine abandon. 'Playing with the angels again!' we cried.

THE NEST

This piece forms a pair with the previous one, taking up some of its ideas and images and developing them further. Its inspiration comes from my own watching of birds, and more significantly from the biblical image of God as a mother bird sheltering her young, a metaphor given perhaps its most beautiful expression in Psalm 17.8, 'Guard me as the apple of the eye; hide me in the shadow of your wings.'

God takes all the cold that is coming,
the cold held tight in the fist of the night
and hurled with such fearful force.

Oh, fearful, yes!
We have every reason to be afraid.
This cold would kill us without her.
We do not yet have angels' wings,
nor their covering of glistening feathers.
This down of ours is not enough
to keep at bay the cutting terrors of the night.
Without her we would die;
the cold would find the spaces in our bones,
and creep inside to occupy our hearts;
our bright eyes would quickly lose their shine.
The nest is perched up high for all to see,
woven tight against the worst of the world's winds,
but not hidden from this cold.
We are too exposed.

So she settles down upon us,
gathers us to the warmth of her brood-patch,
and to the ceaseless beating of her heart.
We have no cause to be afraid!

❧

The day dawns and brings the rain.
No sunshine,
only a lightening of the sky to grey.
The rain is blown off its feet by the storm,
stinging horizontal.
And God takes all the wet that is coming.
She hunkers down in the nest,
hunching out the shoulders of her wings,
lest the wet and the wind smother us instead.
Without her we would die;
wet through in a minute,
frozen to the soul,
we would unconsciously perish.

Yet we are gathered here,
to the warmth of her brood-patch,
and to the ceaseless beating of her heart.
We have no cause to be afraid!

❧

Noon comes, and with it a sun
as fierce as the rain,
as unfeeling as the cold.
We are too exposed;
we cannot escape;
we do not yet have angels' wings;

we cannot leave this small, cramped space of ours.
The sun, left to itself
and its ancient, cruel devices,
would cook us whole
and have us for dinner
before retiring for the night.

But God takes all the heat that is coming.
Beneath her shining wings,
in their deep, cool shadow,
above the ceaseless beating of her heart,
we hear her panting
as if to survive,
like a man struggling for breath
against the driving nails.

∞

Are we imagining things,
or does it really take so much
to bring us to maturity?
Must God indeed endure all this,
until we find our angels' wings
and leave the nest and fly?

ALL IS HOLY

*When I preached this piece in Chester Cathedral, I took as my
text a few words from Hebrews 10.19, 'Since we have confidence
to enter the sanctuary . . .' I have also made use of the parable of
the Good Samaritan in Luke 10.30–37, though I have given
that a fairly vigorous twist.*

The rough-hewn mountains bear his mark,
and ravens weave his spell
about cathedral towers.
Flowers do hold his beauty tight,
and oceans sing his ancient songs.

All is holy.

The child is formed by her inside the womb,
kept safe until the day
of her deliverance.
Laid upon the comfort of her breast,
we grow, we live, we die.

All are holy.

Yet we forget,
as if it's spread too thinly
for our noticing.
We grow too tall and leave
our round-eyed wondering behind.

Yet all is holy.

We treat the world as if it's ours
to push around and bend
into our ways.
Too fascinated by ourselves,
we lack the time to sense

that all is holy.

And when we build deep trenches in our minds,
and sit in them content,
or when we close the bunker's door
for fear of those outside,
we cannot see, we cannot hear

that all are holy.

And when our violence spills into the streets,
or spits its phlegm into our face,
when children die against the guns,
and shouts of angry men
accompany the dead unto the grave

(yet all are holy),

Oh, then we need to bind God's wounds
and raise her up,
and put her on an ass
to bring her to an inn,
and pay the price,

for all are holy.

And if we hold her in our arms,
and dry her tears,

then we will find again
the oldest truth of all,
that all is holy,
bears her mark,
and softly tells her tale.

⚬ↄ

Yet 'all is holy'
seems too grand or too diffuse
for our remembering.
Unless we meet with holy men
and find our holy women on our way,
tuck holy children into bed,
then what will 'all are holy' mean?

We need our spaces, too,
held taught between high walls
and climbing vaults,
so God can fill them with his song,
or curl up small in leafy wood,
or dance with angels on the roof,
or lie quite still in silences immense.

We need the candle flame
to tell us God's at home
and welcoming of all,
with table laid,
and bread upon the plate,
and wine inside the cup
and angels washing up.

And then that ancient truth
might once more creep into our souls,

and bid us cast our heavy boots,
and tread more gently as we go,
and whisper to us,
'All is holy ground;
and all you meet are holy, too.'

∾

'And if the priests start preaching
these bright holy things are theirs
and bar your way into my sanctuary,
or if they say you are too young,
too old, too female, or too bad,
then push them firm out of your way
and pray for them to lose their arrogance.

'And take me with you when you go.'

THE KINGFISHER

20

Over thirty years of birdwatching have filled my head with bright memories. This piece draws on three of them: of standing on a small bridge in Berkshire and being surprised by a kingfisher flying beneath it; of sitting on a Wiltshire hillside on a May evening listening to two nightingales in full song; of watching a peregrine falcon hunting over the Dee estuary near Chester.

If you had been walking along the river, I don't suppose you would have noticed her. A man was fishing just a few yards downstream, and didn't see her. You had to look hard, and know where to look in the first place. But there she was all the same, hidden among the reeds, wonderfully camouflaged, with dappled light playing all about her. God. The God of a universe whose size we cannot begin to imagine, was sitting on the bank of that small, unpretentious river, her beauty compressed within the space of a dove's wing.

On one side of her was a nightingale, on the other a peregrine falcon. These were her archangels. In front of her was a kingfisher, and the kingfisher was speaking. He trembled as he spoke, but not because he was afraid. He had flown a long way that day to speak to his God, and what he had to say was terribly important to him. He had been keeping it to himself. Now he had come to unburden himself.

'Look here, God,' he was saying. 'Look at Michael, your nightingale, or listen to him! Can he sing! Well, you know that, of course, you made him. But have you ever sat and listened to him when he's in full song, really going at it? I dare say you have, come to think of it. It's beautiful, I mean *really* beautiful, isn't it, God? Words don't tell the half of it, do they? You'd never guess to look at him. I mean, no offence, but you wouldn't, would you. He sings angel songs he does, and better than the angels, too.

'Could you make me sing like that, God? I've been trying for a long time, but it comes out all wrong. And while you're about it, could you make me fly like Gabrielle, your peregrine there? I saw a peregrine the other day. Sitting on a post I was, by a stream, where it came out into the estuary, just minding my own business, when one flew over. I kept my head down, I can tell you, but she wasn't interested in me. She kept flying up the beach, only behind it, over the dunes, where the birds feeding out on the mud wouldn't notice her. She seemed to be flying in a lazy sort of way, just strolling on the wind, if you like. And then she turned. Stone me, did she go! She flew straight at the birds on the mud, wings beating hard, hunting speed! They all went up with her in the middle of them. Mayhem it was! I stood there on my little post, just watching. But I lost her in all those swirling birds.

'Could you make me fly like that, God? Nobody takes any notice of me. Just like they don't take any notice of me, when I sing. But if you made me sing like Michael, then all the birds around would stop, and the mother blackbirds and the mother thrushes would say to their young ones, 'Listen to that!' they'd say. 'You might be able to sing like that when you grow up,' they'd say. And then I'd do a bit of flying, and I'd pretend, like that peregrine by the sea, that I didn't mean anything, and I'd go up and up, and then I'd come hurtling down and scare the living daylights out of everyone. It would be marvellous, wouldn't it, God! Can you do it, God? You can do anything, God. Can you do this, God, just for me?'

God laughed. The light about her danced and flashed. The fisherman stayed bent over his rod.

'Turn your head round, my friend, and spread out your wings. Can you see your back?'

The kingfisher tried. 'Not very well,' he said. 'It's too close.'

'Pity. Can you fly upside-down above the water and see your reflection?'

'Pardon? I wouldn't care to try that. Anyway, God, what are you getting at?'

'Just fly upstream for a way, and then turn and fly back here. We'll watch you as you go, Michael, Gabrielle and I.' She laughed again as the kingfisher hesitated. 'Go on,' she said.

The kingfisher did as he was asked, though he didn't have a clue what his God was on about. He flew fast and straight, while the autumn sun shone full on his back, and the blue there caught fire and made all seem dull beside it. He turned and flew back to the patch of light in the reeds.

God clapped her hands. 'My friend, my good friend,' she cried, 'you have your own glory! I have put it on your back! It was a good day's work when I made you! You wear me on your back! Fly now, my kingfisher, flash your blue flame over the water, and we will delight in all that beauty I have given you! You do, you wear me on your back!'

The kingfisher turned his head round again and tried to see. He still found his God hard to believe, but he couldn't refuse her. He gave her one last enquiring look out of his bright eye, then flew off downstream, skimming past the tip of the fisherman's rod.

'Did you catch anything?' the man's wife asked, when he got home.

'Nothing much,' he replied. 'But I saw a kingfisher! Flew right past me it did, the sun right on its back! I'll never forget that. It's been a good day.'

21

BIG ENOUGH FOR GOD TO PLAY

*When I first preached this piece in Chester Cathedral, the set
readings were from Zechariah and Revelation. They included
the words, 'Old men and old women shall again sit in the streets
of Jerusalem . . . and the streets of the city shall be full of boys
and girls playing' (Zechariah 8.4–5), and, 'I saw the holy city,
the new Jerusalem, coming down out of heaven from God'
(Revelation 21.2). Those words set me thinking and put me to
writing.*

*The vision of the heavenly Jerusalem in Revelation comes at
the end of the Bible. Very near the beginning of it is the story
of a garden, the Garden of Eden of Genesis 2—3, and that is
where this piece begins. I make reference, also, to the violence that
Jerusalem has witnessed over the millennia, both to what is spoken
of in the biblical accounts of the Babylonian invasion in the sixth
century BC, and to the troubles of the contemporary city, as well
as to the conditions in which Palestinian and other refugees have
to live.*

At the start
the talk is of a garden
of tempting beauty
and ready fruitfulness,
and water enough
to slake the thirst of all the world.
A garden where paths bear the gleaming marks
of the footsteps of God,
where immortality is for the picking,
where tigers and crocodiles get named
but strike no fear,

where God gets down on hands and knees to
   give us life,
where loneliness is banished by mysterious surgery,
where boy meets girl and breaks into poetry to
   mark his joy,
where life's hardships are beyond the horizon,
where so much, remarkably, is well.

In the end
the vision and its talk have changed.
Now we find ourselves in a city.

That first garden
became a place spoiled by fear and accusation.
Duped by a clever cynic of a snake
the girl and boy grew up too fast,
and learned too soon what adult life would mean.
They found themselves outside the gates,
and when God walked the familiar paths,
as evening breezes stirred the Tree of Life,
no-one heard him any more.

This city has seen far more than that.
The streets and squares where now the weary rest
and watch the children and the angels play,
were once paved with bodies.
Young and old were slaughtered here
and left to rot;
women raped, dirtied with shame,
the blood of babies at their breast.
The sun was hidden by the smoke of its burning,
and its temple,
its holy place,
the house of its impregnable God,

smashed to a pile of rubble
for the snakes to hide in,
and once more catch the unwary.

That and more
Jerusalem has seen with her own eyes.

And now look at her,
basking in the light of God,
cooling her feet in the water from God's seat,
eating her fill of immortality from the Tree of Life,
one vast Holy of Holies,
floodlit by divine glory!

What more could you ask
for the refugees still waiting for permission to
        return?
What more could you dream
for those packed into metal containers in the heat,
who stumble across borders edged with mines,
or pick their way down foreign aircraft steps?
What more could you hope
for those who live as best they can
beneath United Nations flags,
who lean against bare doorways
and walk the pitted streets
of camps within a few hard miles
of our Jerusalem,
who tell you they too come from there,
and name the streets where once they lived,
and talk of work their fathers did?
For them also
what brighter news could you have to bring?

And yet is not a city far too small,
as once a garden,
even Eden,
proved too confined?
Cities have walls,
or peter out in suburb or in shanty town.
Surely no heavenly Jerusalem,
no heaven,
could have any need for walls
to keep its inhabitants in,
or marauders and enemies out?
For marauding and enmity do not threaten heaven,
and why would its people wish to leave?
Surely no heavenly Jerusalem
could circle itself in shanty towns,
for there is no poverty in heaven,
but one equal love,
and one equal dignity and worth.
Surely heaven
can have no boundaries at all,
for God is too large to be so confined,
and God's embrace embraces all,
especially those we think beyond her pale.

Surely heaven is neither city nor garden,
but rather ocean with no floor,
or air without height.
Surely we will all swim and dive and splash
in the ocean of God's love,
or launch ourselves
and ride the air of her delight.

Surely heaven is big enough for God to play.